S0-ABD-562

Hesperia Branch Library

9650 7th Avenue

Hesperia, CA 92345

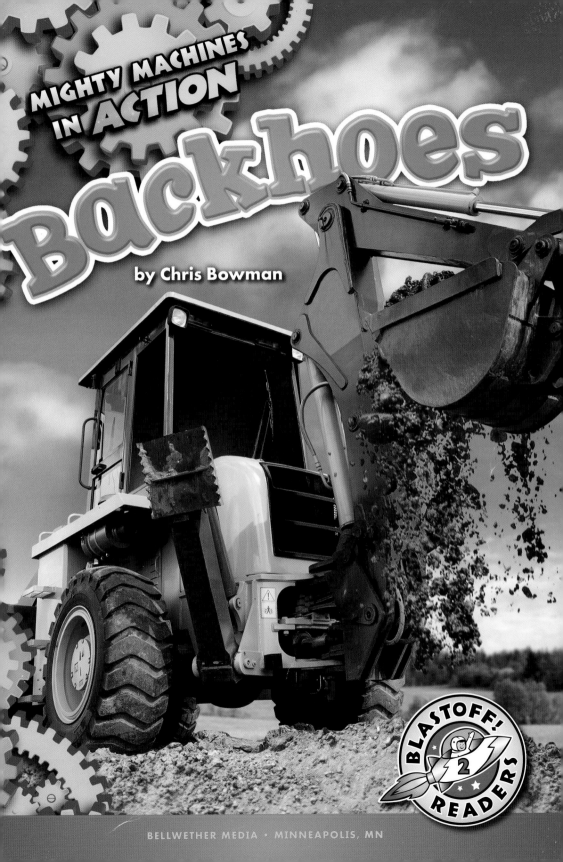

MIGHTY MACHINES IN ACTION

Backhoes

by Chris Bowman

BELLWETHER MEDIA · MINNEAPOLIS, MN

BLASTOFF! 2 READERS

Note to Librarians, Teachers, and Parents:

Blastoff! Readers are carefully developed by literacy experts and combine standards-based content with developmentally appropriate text.

Level 1 provides the most support through repetition of high-frequency words, light text, predictable sentence patterns, and strong visual support.

Level 2 offers early readers a bit more challenge through varied simple sentences, increased text load, and less repetition of high-frequency words.

Level 3 advances early-fluent readers toward fluency through increased text and concept load, less reliance on visuals, longer sentences, and more literary language.

Level 4 builds reading stamina by providing more text per page, increased use of punctuation, greater variation in sentence patterns, and increasingly challenging vocabulary.

Level 5 encourages children to move from "learning to read" to "reading to learn" by providing even more text, varied writing styles, and less familiar topics.

Whichever book is right for your reader, Blastoff! Readers are the perfect books to build confidence and encourage a love of reading that will last a lifetime!

This edition first published in 2017 by Bellwether Media, Inc.

No part of this publication may be reproduced in whole or in part without written permission of the publisher. For information regarding permission, write to Bellwether Media, Inc., Attention: Permissions Department, 5357 Penn Avenue South, Minneapolis, MN 55419.

Library of Congress Cataloging-in-Publication Data

Names: Bowman, Chris, author.
Title: Backhoes / by Chris Bowman.
Description: Minneapolis, MN : Bellwether Media, Inc., [2017] | Series: Blastoff! Readers. Mighty Machines in Action | Audience: Ages 5-8. | Audience: K to grade 3. | Includes bibliographical references and index.
Identifiers: LCCN 2016032047 (print) | LCCN 2016033097 (ebook) | ISBN 9781626176003 (hardcover : alk. paper) | ISBN 9781681033303 (ebook)
Subjects: LCSH: Backhoes–Juvenile literature.
Classification: LCC TA735 .B67 2017 (print) | LCC TA735 (ebook) | DDC 629.225–dc23
LC record available at https://lccn.loc.gov/2016032047

Text copyright © 2017 by Bellwether Media, Inc. BLASTOFF! READERS and associated logos are trademarks and/or registered trademarks of Bellwether Media, Inc. SCHOLASTIC, CHILDREN'S PRESS, and associated logos are trademarks and/or registered trademarks of Scholastic Inc.

Editor: Christina Leighton   Designer: Steve Porter

Printed in the United States of America, North Mankato, MN.

Table of Contents

DIG DEEP

A backhoe drives up to a group of trees. A farmer wants to clear them to make a pond.

First, the backhoe digs around the trees.

Then the backhoe presses
against the trees. They fall over!

The backhoe pulls them away.
Now it is ready to dig the pond.

MANY JOBS

Backhoes are often found on farms or **construction sites**.

They dig **ditches** or large holes. They also move rocks and dirt.

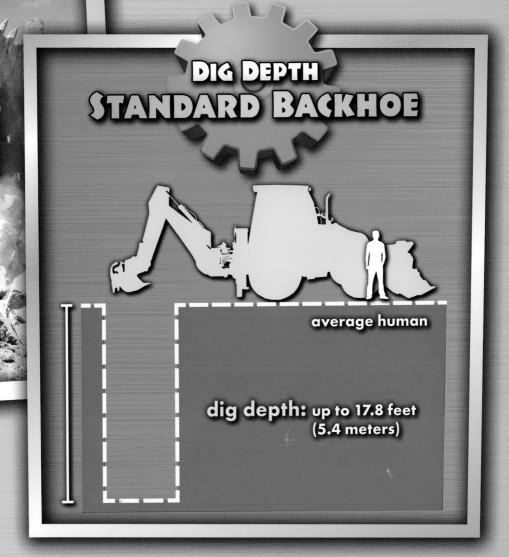

Dig Depth
STANDARD BACKHOE

average human

dig depth: up to 17.8 feet
(5.4 meters)

Backhoes also break things down. Some tear down buildings.

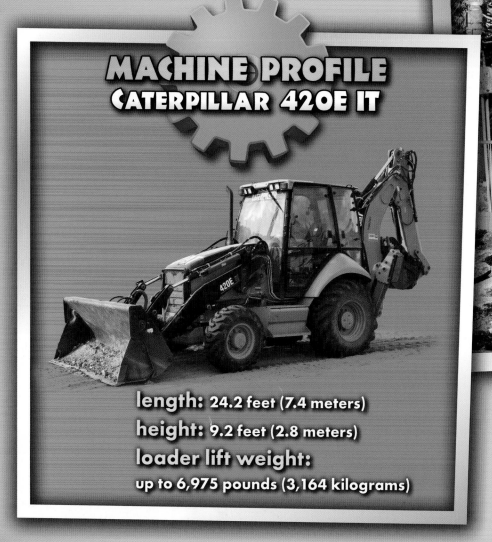

MACHINE PROFILE
CATERPILLAR 420E IT

length: 24.2 feet (7.4 meters)
height: 9.2 feet (2.8 meters)
loader lift weight:
up to 6,975 pounds (3,164 kilograms)

Others work on roads. They break up the old surface. Then they spread the new **asphalt**.

The **loader** is on the front of the machine. It works like a big shovel.

loader

It lifts, carries, and spreads dirt and rocks.

The **tractor** connects to the loader. It holds the **diesel engine**.

tractor

cab

The driver sits in the **cab**.
The chair can face forward
or backward.

The backhoe is behind the tractor. It looks like an arm with a **bucket** on the end.

backhoe

It digs into the ground
and lifts heavy objects.

Backhoes move on all types of ground. Their big wheels do not get stuck on rocks or in sand.

Their powerful engines **rumble** loudly.

IDENTIFY A
BACKHOE

tractor

loader

bucket

leg

When it is time to dig, two legs keep the backhoe in place.

These balance the machine.
Then it gets the job done!

Glossary

asphalt—a material used to make roads

bucket—a scoop on the end of the backhoe

cab—the part of the tractor where the driver sits

construction sites—places where things are built

diesel engine—a loud engine that burns diesel fuel and is often used in big machines

ditches—long holes in the ground; ditches often hold or move water.

loader—a big shovel on the front of the tractor

rumble—to make a low sound

tractor—a powerful machine that pulls or carries equipment

To Learn More

AT THE LIBRARY

Clay, Kathryn. *Backhoes*. North Mankato, Minn.: Capstone Press, 2017.

Lennie, Charles. *Excavators*. Minneapolis, Minn.: Abdo Kids, 2015.

Osier, Dan. *Backhoes*. New York, N.Y.: PowerKids Press, 2014.

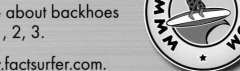

ON THE WEB

Learning more about backhoes is as easy as 1, 2, 3.

1. Go to www.factsurfer.com.

2. Enter "backhoes" into the search box.

3. Click the "Surf" button and you will see a list of related web sites.

With factsurfer.com, finding more information is just a click away.

Index

The images in this book are reproduced through the courtesy of: Dmitry Kalinovsky, front cover; Michael Melnikoff, p. 4 (background); Jorgosphotos, p. 4 (backhoe); Vlue, pp. 4-5, 6-7; gece33, pp. 8, 20-21; Maria Jeffs, pp. 10, 16-17 (left); Natalia Rakowska, pp. 10-11; Alaettin YILDIRIM, p. 12; kadmy, pp. 12-13; Ivto, p. 14; Russ Lickteig, p. 15; cyran, pp. 16-17 (right); ewg3D, pp. 18-19; Yury Gubin, p. 19; HumongoNationphotogallery, p. 19 (inset); gece33, pp. 20-21.

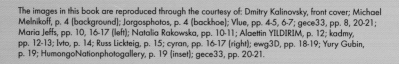